I DEDICATE THIS BOOK TO BETTY BASSEY (Aunty B) MY OLDER SISTER WHO I SHARED PRELIMINARY IDEAS OF THIS BOOK BUT PASSED ON TO GLORY BEFORE IT CAME TO LIFE.

**WRITTEN BY
LILIAN RUACH**

**ILLUSTRATED BY
DENZEL ERINNE**

FIRST THING IN
THE MORNING?

BRUSH MY TEETH,
BEFORE I EAT

WHEN YOU ARE SEATED
AT THE DINNING
TABLE

EAT MY CEREAL
WHILE I READ THE
LABEL

WHEN YOU GET INTO
THE SCHOOL BUS

I'LL SAY HI
TO THE DRIVER,
AND I WON'T
MAKE A FUSS

IF YOUR FRIEND COMES
TO SCHOOL WITHOUT
A SNACK

I'LL GIVE THEM A PIECE FROM MY PACK
1+1=2
2+2=4
4+4=8
Elephant

WHEN YOU GET BULLIED
IN SCHOOL

A B C D E F G
H I J K L M N O
P Q R S T U V W X
Y Z
LET MY TEACHER KNOW HE IS BEING CRUEL

AT HOME WITH YOUR HOMEWORK

I'LL FINISH UP
AND GET SOME
SNACKS IN
MY STOMACH

WHEN YOUR LITTLE SISTER
WANTS TO PLAY WITH
YOUR TOYS

SHARING IS THE
RIGHT CHOICE

WHEN MAMA SAYS TO
TAKE A NAP

ZZZZZZZzzz
I'LL GO TO BED,
AND CALL IT A WRAP

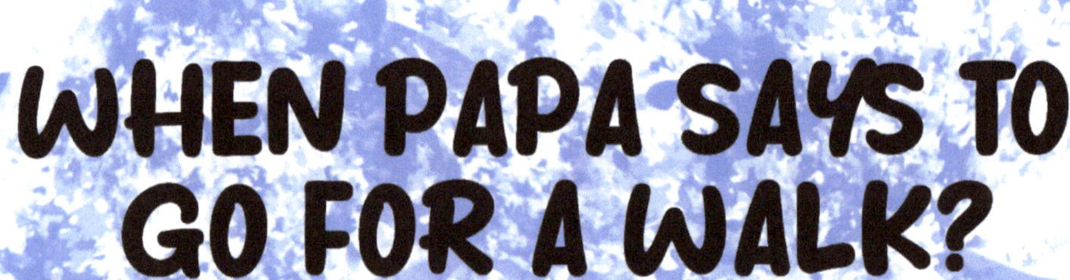
WHEN PAPA SAYS TO
GO FOR A WALK?

A WALK IS
ALWAYS A NICE
TIME TO TALK

AFTER YOU USE THE
BATHROOM?

WASHING MY HANDS, IS THE NUMBER ONE RULE

WHEN YOUR FRIENDS
COME OVER FOR
A PLAY DATE?

PLAYING WITH
MY FRIENDS
IS ALWAYS GREAT

WHEN YOUR BABY
SISTER
IS CRYING AND MAMA
IS BUSY

I'LL ROCK HER TO SLEEP, IT'S SO EASY

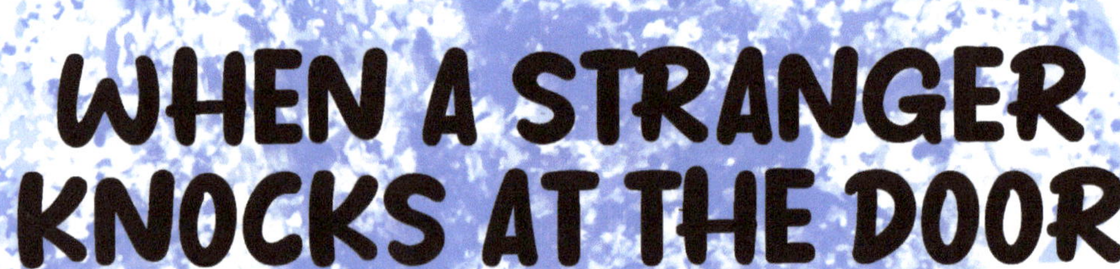

WHEN A STRANGER KNOCKS AT THE DOOR

Knock
Knock
Knock
NEVER ANSWER THE DOOR IF YOU ARE UNSURE

WHEN A STRANGER
COMES TOWARDS YOU
AND OFFERS
YOU A TREAT

I SAY NO AND I RETREAT

WHEN IT'S TIME TO
TAKE A SHOWER

IT FEELS GOOD
AND IT DOESN'T TAKE
AN HOUR

WHAT WILL YOU DO
IF YOU MEET
THE PRESIDENT

I'LL GIVE HIM
A HUG AND SOME
CANDY AS
A PRESENT

ABOUT THE AUTHOR

Lilian Ruach is a children's book author known for her imaginative and informative stories that capture the hearts and minds of children around the world.

Lilian found her love for stories while working as a child care worker with over 3 decades of experience before she became an author and a healthcare provider.

Lilian writes stories that teaches kids valuable life lessons and morals while simultaneously entertaining them, drawing on her experiences as a caregiver.

Lilian Ruach is revered in the field of children's literature for her imaginative energy and persistent dedication to uplifting and encouraging children.